THE NATURAL SUPERIORITY OF THE LEFT-HANDER

THE NATURAL SUPERIORITY OF THE LEFT-HANDER

JAMES T. de KAY

ANGUS
& ROBERTSON
PUBLISHERS

ANGUS & ROBERTSON PUBLISHERS

Unit 4, Eden Park, 31 Waterloo Road,
North Ryde, NSW, Australia 2113, and
16 Golden Square, London WIR 4BN,
United Kingdom

First published in the United States
by M. Evans and Company, Inc.
as The Left-Handed Book *in 1966,*
and The Natural Superiority of the Left-Hander *in 1979*
This combined edition first published in Australia
by Angus & Robertson Publishers in 1986
First published in the United Kingdom
by Angus & Robertson (UK) Ltd in 1986

Copyright © 1966, 1979 by James T. de Kay
Copyright © this adaptation 1986
by James T. de Kay
Published by arrangement with
M. Evans and Company, Inc., New York

National Library of Australia
Cataloguing-in-publication data.

De Kay, James T.
  The natural superiority of the left-hander.

  ISBN 0 207 15349 3.

  1. Left and right-handedness — Caricatures and
  cartoons. 2. American wit and humor, Pictorial.
  I. Title.

741.5'973

Printed in Singapore

Dedicated to Alexander the Great, Benjamin Franklin, Babe Ruth, Hans Holbein, Betty Grable, Rock Hudson, Peter Lawford, Rudy Vallee, Joanne Woodward, Dick Van Dyke, Judy Garland, Charlemagne, Pablo Picasso, King George VI, Lord Nelson, Joan of Arc, Billy the Kid, Rod Laver, Martina Navratilova, John McEnroe, Jimi Hendrix and half the Beatles (Paul and Ringo), who are all left-handed, and to Gareth de Kay, who is not.

One person in ten is a left-
hander. And all of them think
they're sort of special.

Which is probably true . . .

No kidding. Anywhere you look, left-handedness is something of a rarity.
Even most plants are right-handed. Honeysuckle is one of the few climbing plants that twines to the left.

It could be that the only case where left-handers are in the majority is among gorillas. Their left arms outweigh their right, which may indicate a slight left-handed bias. But that's only speculation.

As far as human beings are concerned, as we know from cave drawings, in the early days there were plenty of right-handers, but there were plenty of left-handers, too.

If Neanderthal men were exclusively right-handed, they would have invented right-handed tools, correct? Instead, they invented **ambidextrous** tools, suitable for either hand:

hammers,

saws,

axes,

pails,

pottery,

Obviously, a lot of left-handed Neanderthals helped design these clever innovations.

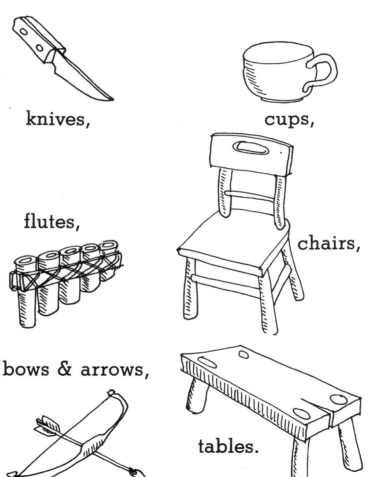

knives,

cups,

flutes,

chairs,

bows & arrows,

tables.

Throughout much of ancient history, the left-handers had equal rights:

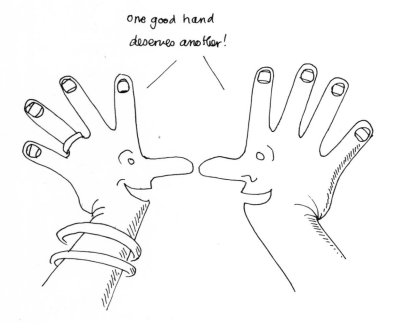

one good hand
deserves another!

This was even true in writing . . .

The Egyptians didn't feel they had to write left to right. They wrote up, down, left **or** right, depending on whim.

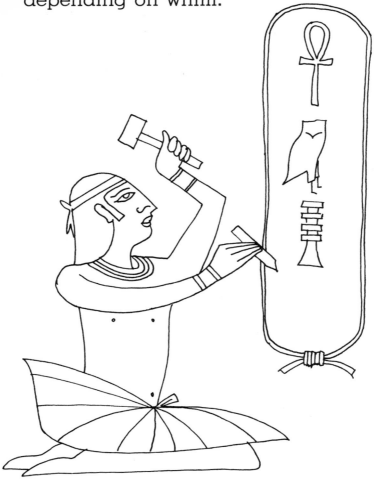

The Greeks wrote BOUSTRO-
PHEDON style, with each line
alternating down the page, like an
ox plowing a field:
first line left to right,
next line right to left,
then another left to right
etc.etc.

The Chinese, even to this day, write in vertical columns from right to left, which would indicate a slightly left-handed preference.